SOMEDAY I'M GOING TO MARRY KATY PERRY

Available from University of Hell Press:

by Eirean Bradley
the I in team

by Calvero
someday i'm going to marry Katy Perry

by Brian S. Ellis
American Dust Revisited

by Greg Gerding
The Burning Album of Lame
Venue Voyeurisms: Bars of San Diego
Loser Makes Good: Selected Poems 1994
Piss Artist: Selected Poems 1995-1999
The Idiot Parade: Selected Poems 2000-2005

by Lindsey Kugler
HERE.

by Johnny No Bueno
We Were Warriors

by Stephen M. Park
High & Dry

someday i'm going to marry Katy Perry

by Calvero

illustrations by Nation of Amanda

This book published by University of Hell Press.
www.universityofhellpress.com

Book Design by Vince Norris
www.norrisportfolio.com

Cover & Illustrations by Nation of Amanda
nationofamanda.tumblr.com

Some of these pieces first appeared in online literary journals *The Legendary*, *Danse Macabre*, *Haggard & Halloo*, *HorrorSleazeTrash*, and *The Writing Disorder.*

Published in the United States of America.
ISBN 978-1-938753-04-6

Table of Contents

CHAPTER TWO

CHAPTER THREE

This book is dedicated to my father.

I hope he doesn't think it sucks.

CHAPTER ONE

energy drinks and diet sodas

I like energy drinks.
I like diet sodas too.

They both taste good
and therefore I drink both of them
quite frequently,
especially diet soda.

Because I drink so many
energy drinks
and because I drink
so many diet sodas
I have to pee quite a bit
throughout the day.

Pissing so much
throughout the day
might annoy most people
but I really don't mind it.
I don't mind it at all
actually.

I like taking pisses,
especially long ones.

Sometimes when I have to pee
I hold it in
for as long as I can.
This way my pisses last longer
coming out.
I like taking long pisses.
They feel extra good
as they spray out of me
and into the toilet.

I spend most of my day
feeling nothing at all,
and when I do finally feel something

it's usually something
pretty horrible like
sadness,
frustration,
hopelessness,
embarrassment,
aggravation,
anxiety,
shame,
dread.

But the long pisses make me feel good.
They're an amazing release.
They're like a longer
but much more mild orgasm.
Plus I don't have to chase
or beg
or buy some girl dinner
or drinks
to get one.
That and I don't need to repay the favor
and have my face
stuck between her legs
for forty-five minutes,
tracing designs
all over her crotch
with the tip of my tongue
as she squirms
and writhes
and continually tells me how close she is.
(I'm either really bad at it
or really good at it.
I'm not sure yet
which one
though.)

No,
all I need to do
to feel good

when I don't have any other reason
to feel good
is drink an energy drink
        or a diet soda
and then eventually
I'll take a piss
and feel good again
inside.

It's never much
and it never lasts for long
but only when you're able
to find small amounts
of happiness
loitering in the shadows
and cowering in the darkness
will you ever be able to find it
anywhere else.

That's why I drink
energy drinks
and diet sodas.

        That and they taste
            really good
                too.

all of the best pickpockets sniff their own farts

During my lunch break
I sat in my car
and my car was parked
in a large,
half empty
parking lot
and no one knew
where I was
and no one knew
what I was doing
and the people
and the cars
and the world
were racing past
outside of my car
and as everything raced past
outside of my car
I felt removed
from it all,
    from the people,
    from the cars,
    from the whole planet,
and then
my butthole
began to tingle.
It began to tingle
and it felt just like
when I was little
and I'd play
hide and seek
and I'd be hiding
and my butthole
would begin to tingle
because I'd found
such an amazing
hiding spot
where I knew no one

would ever find me,
and there was
this excitement
that I was getting away
with something,
and there was this
dread and nervous
anticipation
that I'd somehow
be found
when I really didn't want
to be found,
and as I sat there
in my car
I could feel it
out there …
I could feel
the world
out there
and that it was looking for me
and trying to find me,
        but somehow,
                through shit luck,
I had stumbled upon
this amazing
hiding spot
in my car
in this large,
half empty
parking lot.

I heard the world
whizzing by
outside of my car
and I could feel it
looking for me
so I slouched down
into my seat
and tried
to keep quiet.

I *tried*
to keep quiet,
but whenever
I'm supposed to keep quiet
is always when
I get a case
of the giggles,
so I slouched further down
into my seat
and I began giggling
to myself.
I began giggling
to myself like,
    hehehehehehehehehehe ...
I giggled
to myself
real girlish-like
and no matter
how hard I tried
I couldn't hold it in.
Then I began
laughing,
    full-on guffawing
    you could say,
and I went ...
    A-HAHAHAHAHAHAHAHAHA
    HAHA!
I laughed so hard
a little pee
came out of
my pee hole
and that was when
I realized
I had to pee.
    That always
happened to me
too
whenever I played
hide and seek.
    I'd find this

amazing hiding spot
and then out of nowhere
I'd suddenly have to pee
as badly
as a race horse
with a baby bladder.

I had to pee
real bad
but I had
such a good hiding spot
that I knew I couldn't
leave my car.
If I left my car
the world
would find me
and I didn't want that.
I didn't want that
at all
so I grabbed an empty
McDonald's cup
and I unzipped my fly
and I whipped out my dick
and I began peeing
into the cup
right there
in my car.
Luckily
it was a large size
soda fountain cup
because I peed
a lot.
        A whole lot.
Then I placed
the cup full of pee
in a cup holder
and made a mental note
that there was pee
in that cup
and not to drink from it

because I don't like
drinking pee.

After I peed
I felt better.
        I felt relieved
                too.
I felt relieved
because I let
a lot of pee out
and because
I hadn't given up
my bitchin'
hiding spot
and the world
still hadn't found me,
        and I didn't want
the world
to find me
because the world
is stupid
and it grinds you down
and it steals from you.
It steals
your energy
and your passions
and,
        worst of all,
                your time.
It just takes,
                takes,
                        takes
away from you
and it rushes you
and pushes you
and it shoves you
along
and the world
just takes,
                takes,

takes
and it's a no good
dirty thief
and it wears you down
and grinds you down
until your poor,
old body
just can't take
the futility of it
anymore.

But the world
wasn't stealing from me
because it couldn't
find me.
That moment
in time was mine,
alllllllll mine
because I was hidden,
hidden away
from the stupid,
thieving,
conniving
world
and then I realized
I had to fart
so I did.
I farted
and that fart
was mine
too
and the world
was never going to get
its grubby hands
on it.
That fart was mine
so I breathed
it in.
I breathed it in
nice and deep

too
and I filled
my lungs
with it
and as I filled
my lungs
with it
I could've sworn
I heard my lungs scream,
    "Dude! Gross!
        What the fuck
        are you doing out there?
            Stop it!!!"
But I didn't care,
and even though
I never particularly
enjoyed the smell
of my own farts
I did right there
in that moment,
and even though
I was a guy
who had just peed
in an empty
McDonald's cup
and who was sitting
all alone
in his shitbox
of a car
and who was sniffing in
and breathing in
and enjoying the smell
of his own farts
I felt like
a winner,
    like a miraculous
champion,
and I pretended
to pin a blue ribbon
on my chest

and then I looked up
at the blue sky
and the clouds looked like
big-breasted, hot women
made out of marshmallows
and they were all
on their backs
and had their legs spread
wide open
and their vaginas
were smiling
and winking
at me
and then I began
to blush,
but even though
I began
to blush
I still felt like
a winner,
        like a miraculous
champion,

and I was.

At that moment
I
really,
really
was.

Small,
selfish
victories
like sniffing
and enjoying
your own farts
will take you further
than most friendships,
than most loves

ever will.

Learn
to become
a pickpocket.

Learn
to steal back
from the world
that steals
so much
from you.

the racist viking (so sleepy)

I've always been
a real viking
when it comes to eating.
I devour my food
almost instantly.
I go
Nom, nom, nom!
and then my food is gone
just like that.
You probably wish
you were as good at eating
as I am
but you're not.
I'm the best.
        Sorry.

One afternoon
not too long ago
I had just victoriously
polished off my lunch
at this favorite fast food place
of mine.
I went
Nom, nom, nom!
and my lunch was gone
just like that
just like always.
I was real proud
of myself too
just like I usually
am.

Sitting in the booth across from me
there was a man
eating his lunch.
He was sitting alone
just like me
but he wasn't as good at eating

as me.
Not even close.

The man
was a black man,
        a very big black man.
                Not *fat* kind of big.
                        More girthy than anything,
                                and tall too,
and with his large stature
he should have been very good at eating
but he wasn't.
I was better.
I don't like to brag
but I was.
I should've gone over there
and talked to him
and given him some pointers;
Open your mouth wider.
        Take bigger bites.
                Don't chew. Just swallow.
It was a real amateur hour
over there.
I should've helped him
but I didn't want to
although
I wasn't sure
why.
So he just sat there
taking modest bites
out of his cheeseburger
eating it all wrong
while I sipped my diet soda
and watched him eat
out of the corner of my eye.

As I watched him
I slowly came to
the realization as to why
I didn't want to help him:

I hated him.
I don't think I hated him
because he was black.
No,
that wasn't it.
That wasn't it at all.
I didn't hate him
because he was black.
That would mean I'm racist
and racist people
are fucking assholes
and should be herded
into rockets
and shot into the sun.
No,
that's not me.
I'm not a racist.
I didn't hate him
because he was black.
I hated him because
he was human.

I am human too
apparently
although I never come close
to feeling like one.
Don't get me wrong,
I do a lot of things that
most normal humans beings
do; I eat,
sleep,
crap,
piss,
fart,
curse,
weep.
I pick lint
out of my bellybutton.
I watch my cats
shit in their litter boxes,

but still,
even when doing all these typical
human things
I never feel much
like one of them.
Not even
close.

So I just sat there
hating that guy
who didn't know how to eat.
I was good at that too,
hating that is,
a real viking,
just like I was with eating,
but shit
was it exhausting.
It was making me tired.
Real tired.
I couldn't believe
how much energy it took
just to dislike someone
so strongly.

I better stop,
I thought,
or else
I'm going to fall asleep
right here,
right now.

So I sat there
and I waited for myself
to stop hating him.
I waited
and waited
and waited.
I waited a long time
but I couldn't do it.
I couldn't stop.

I hated that man.
Not because he was black
but because he was human
and because he most likely
felt human
too
and I didn't.

I hated him
because I felt
so disconnected
from something
I was innately
supposed to be.

Amidst my hating
a fat Spanish woman
sat down in the booth
next to mine
and began eating her food.
I hated her too,
and wouldn't you know it,
that made me
even more tired.

And then
minutes later,
an entire family
of four sat down
in the far corner
of the restaurant.
They all looked
really happy together.
I really hated them.
So much so
I could barely
keep my eyes
open.

Holy shit …

I better leave ...
right ... now ...
or else ......
I ...... might
fall ....

"Hey you!
Wake up!"

I startled awake.
The manager
of the place was
standing over me.
He looked down at me
with fuzzy, furrowed,
twitching eyebrows.
I had no idea how long
I'd been out.

"You can't sleep
in here!"
the manager yelled.
"What are you?
Some bum?
If you wanna sleep in here
you're gonna have to leave!"

I slowly stood up
and grabbed my coat.

"Hey ...
have you ever
heard of anyone
being crammed
into a rocket
and shot
into the sun?"
I asked him.

"What? ... No.

Why?"

"No reason,"
I told him.

And then I walked out,
walked to my car,
drove home
and took
a nap.

zzzzzzzzzzzzzzzzz ...

today a tree waved at me

Today
a tree
waved at me.

I really
appreciated it
because today
was a bad day.

Today
was a *really*
bad day.

Today
was one of those days
when you feel
so alone
that all of the people
around you
transform into squirrels
and you see them
scurrying past you
out of the corner
of your eye
but you don't really pay
any attention to them
because,
    "Hey,
    they're just squirrels,"
and sure they're there
but they might as well
not be
because they don't concern you.
    They're just squirrels,
and you don't talk
to squirrels
or touch them
or even approach them

because they're squirrels
and you're not.

That's why
I really appreciated it
when the tree
waved at me.
I felt really bad
though
because I didn't wave back.
I wasn't trying
to be rude
or anything.
It's just that
I was really embarrassed
because when the tree
waved at me
I had just stuffed
two acorns
into my mouth
and I got self-conscious
that the tree saw me
doing so,
that the tree saw me
trying to fit in
with the squirrels
so I didn't
wave back.

Then I felt guilty
that I didn't wave back,
like the tree
was judging me
and thinking
that I was some kind of
rude, unappreciative asshole
or something
so I felt the need
to try and make up for
the fact

that I didn't wave back
but I overcompensated
and I winked
at the tree
and then I was pretty sure
that the tree thought
I was trying to hit on him
or that I was slutty
which totally
wasn't the case.

Okay,
maybe I'm a little bit
slutty
but I'm not, like,
tree slutty
or anything.

I just never should've
popped those acorns
into my mouth.

Being yourself
in a world
full of squirrels
is the hardest thing
you'll ever
have to do.

Then I got nervous
because I didn't want the tree
to think
that I thought
he was ugly
or fat
or something.
The last thing
I ever wanna do
is give a tree

an eating disorder.
So, in order
to make sure
that I didn't ruin
the tree's body image,
I went over to the tree
and began dry humping him
so he'd feel good
about himself.
And as I dry humped him
to make sure he'd feel good
about himself
I saw all the squirrels
watching me
with confused,
raised eyebrows
and I was like,
Awwww shit …
As if they didn't think
I was weird enough
already.

Being yourself
in a world
full of squirrels
is the hardest thing
you'll ever
have to do.

Maybe I am
just a little bit
tree slutty …

I hope
the people
actually look like
people
tomorrow.

freak show

Sometimes
I wish I had been born
with a dildo
on my head.
Especially one
that comically
wobbled
back and forth
whenever I walked.

That'd be great.

Or sometimes
I wish I had been born
with a third arm
shooting straight
out of my ass
and instead of a hand
I just had a tiny
boombox
on the end of my arm
that played nothing but
Creed
over
and over
and over.
Or sometimes
I wish I had been born
with vagina lips
on my mouth
instead of these regular
lips I have now
and with a dog's snout
with a cold,
rubbery, wet
black nose
instead of this

plain old,
boring,
normal nose.
Or sometimes
I wish I had been born
a different color, like
purple
or red
or blue
or green
or periwinkle
or teal.
Any one of those
would be fine
with me.
    I'm not picky.

Man …
It really would have been great
to have been born with any one
of those deformities,
to have something
so freakishly wrong
with me.
People would've
stared at me,
spat at me,
laughed at me,
ridiculed me,
bullied me.
It would've been amazing.
    Well,
maybe not amazing,
but at least then
I would've had a reason as to why
I itch
for isolation,
why I crave
solitude.
Because now

people don't
stare at me,
spit at me,
laugh at me,
ridicule me
or
bully me
and still
all I want is to be
all alone,
all alone,
all alone
all the time,

and you know what that means:

that means there's
      really
something
wrong with me.

the dolphins of the sky

I eat
when I'm unhappy
and yesterday
I was eating a cheeseburger
on a bench
at a park
because I
          was
unhappy
and as I was eating
my cheeseburger
a pigeon
fluttered down
and began
walking around
in front of my feet.
After watching him
for a bit
I realized
he wasn't walking.
He was strutting
more than anything else
   really
and all I could think was,
I bet
that pigeon
is happier
than I am,
and that thought
made me upset.
   Angry even.

So I told
the pigeon,
   I told him right out loud, I told him,
"You're not that great,
you know.
   You're really not …

Do you know
what people call you
and your kind?
They call you
rats with wings.
Mmm hmm. You heard me.
Rats with wings.
  Yep …
How do you like that?"

And then the pigeon
stopped strutting.
His strut
turned into
a somber walk
and then I felt bad.

I felt like
a douche.

I felt like
the douchiest douche
that ever did
douche.

"I'm sorry,"
I said to the pigeon.
"That was
uncalled for.
I didn't mean it,
  and for what it's worth,
I don't think
you're a rat with wings.
I think you
and your kind
are very majestic
and friendly.
You guys
are like the dolphins
of the sky,"

I told him.

The pigeon looked
at me
and then
he went,
  "*COOOO! COOOO!*"
and then
he flew away.

And even though
my Pigeon
is a little bit rusty,
I still knew exactly
what he said
to me.

All
of your days
aren't going to be
happy days
and some days
all you can do
is try not to be
the person
who gets,
  "You know what?
Just because
you're an unhappy,
chubby,
miserable
fuckhead
doesn't give you
the right
to take your shitty life
out on me!"
yelled at you
by a pigeon.

You're right,

Mr. Pigeon.

I'm sorry.

Or should I say … ?
"*COO COOOOO!*
COOO!"

saint black man

I held the door
for an older
black gentleman
when I was going into
McDonald's
and as I held
the door for him
he stopped,
looked me
in the eye,
and smiled
the biggest smile
at me
I had ever seen.
It was so warm
it almost
melted my face
off,
like a flame thrower.

This older
black dude
had a flame thrower
smile
and it went,
Whoooooosh!!!
with scorching friendliness
and it almost
melted my face
off
but it didn't.

Then
he said to me,
"By the grace of God,
young man,
thank you!
Thank you

so kindly!"
Then
he graciously
tipped his hat
to me
like a really cool
cowboy
and he moseyed on
inside.

That man
was
a saint.

I didn't know
his name
so I dubbed him
St. Black Man,
patron saint
of smiles
and really cool
cowboy
hat tipping,

and he was beautiful,
  that St. Black Man,
    like the Mona Lisa,
except he was a dude,
and he was black,
and he had short hair,
and he wasn't made
of paint
either.

I got behind him
in line.
He ordered
a 4-piece Chicken McNugget
and a small fry
to go.

Then he got his food,
walked out
of the place
and got into his car.
Then his car
transformed
into a spaceship
and he flew
up and away
into outer space.
No one else
seemed to notice him
flying away
into outer space though,
        but I did
and all I could think was,

        Yeah …
That actually makes
a lot of sense.

Then
it was my turn
to order.
I got
a 4-piece Chicken McNugget
and a small fry
to go
because idols
walk among us
every day
and unlike the ones
under bright lights
and unlike the ones
dressed in gold
it's usually the ones
in disguise
that are worth
worshipping.

That's why
when I grow up
I wanna be
just like
St. Black Man.

I better
start practicing
my smiling
and cool cowboy
hat tipping now
though.

my dad is a genius and this poem kind of has a dumb and dumber reference in it and my dad loves dumb and dumber further proving that he is, in fact, a genius

I was
picking up garbage
out in front of
where I work
and the place
where I work
is on a really busy street
where dozens of cars
whiz by
every couple of seconds
and there I am
picking up garbage
and as I picked up garbage
I could feel
all those drivers
gazing at me
and judging me
and saying
to themselves,
        Man …
would you look
at that poor,
pathetic,
bastard
picking up trash.
I dunno
what kind of
shitty-ass choices
he must've made
in his life
to end up doing that
for a living
but I kinda wanna
pull over

and ask him
just to make sure
I never make
the same ones ...

And I could feel
all of them
looking at me
and judging me
and laughing at me
and even the Hispanic dude
across the street
who was dressed up
as Lady Liberty
and handing out flyers
for some insurance company
seemed to be smirking
at me
and secretly laughing
at me
and lucky for him
he was dressed up
as Lady Liberty
or else I would've marched
right across the street
and slugged him
right in his
cross-dressing lip,
    and nice and hard
too,
    but I didn't.
I didn't slug him
right in his
cross-dressing lip
because I was already
"the poor bastard
who picks up garbage
for a living"
and I didn't wanna be
"the unpatriotic asshole

who slugged Lady Liberty
in the lip
AND
the poor bastard
who picks up garbage
for a living."

I didn't
wanna be
that guy …

Who would
wanna party
with that guy?

So I just walked around
out in front of my job
picking up
piece of trash
after
piece of trash
and I even found
a tiny, little,
white pill
on the sidewalk
and I was like,
Dear Lord,
please let this be
a cyanide capsule,
so I popped it
in my mouth
but it didn't kill me
and then I was like,
"Aw, shucks …"
and I'm still not
exactly sure
what the pill was for
although lately
I have been feeling
some tenderness

around my breasts,
but at the same time
they are a lot more
supple than usual,
    so hey,
at least
I've got that
going for me.

But the pill
wasn't cyanide
and it didn't kill me
which meant I had to
keep picking up trash
as the world whizzed by
witnessing
my culmination
of failures
and my
collection
of mistakes
which had led me
to where I was
at that very garbage-picking moment,
    and we're all
just a culmination of failures
and a collection
of mistakes
but the difference
between me
and everyone else
is that everyone else
seems to learn
from their failures
and their mistakes
and I never do
and all I could think
as the whole world
seemed to whiz by me
and laugh at me

was,
... That Louis Armstrong's
full of shit,
man,
and right then and there
I had the most
incredible urge
to just pull down
my pants
so every time
I bent over
to pick up garbage
the drivers wouldn't see me
picking up garbage.
They'd just see
my big, white ass
staring at them
like hairy eyeballs
with no pupils,
and instead of saying
to themselves,
Would you look
at that poor,
pathetic,
bastard
picking up trash,
they'd say,
Would you look
at that crazy
son of a bitch
with his bare ass out
in the open
like that,
because I'd rather be
"that crazy,
insane
son of a bitch
with his bare ass out
in the open
like that"

than
"that poor,
pathetic,
bastard
picking up trash."

Then
my shift ended
and I went home
looking absolutely
miserable
as I always did
and my father
saw me
and told me
he loved me
        and for no reason
whatsoever
except for the fact
that my father
is a genius
and he knows
and understands
that facing life
most days
is even scarier
than facing
death.

It took me
until
I was eight
years old
to learn how to
confidently
be able
to tie
my shoes.

Yeah …

I'm pretty sure
I'm
adopted
too.

if i weren't so lazy i'd make a clone of myself so that way i could kill myself

If I weren't so lazy
I'd make a clone
of myself
so that way
I could
kill myself.

The only thing
holding me back
from killing myself
right now
is the sadness
it would cause
to the handful of people
who love me,
    but if I made a clone
of myself
then I wouldn't have to
feel bad
for killing myself
at all.
Nope.
    Not even one bit!
No one would even
have to know
I had killed myself
because my clone
would be there
to take
my place.
So ya see?
It's the perfect plan!

I really want to
make a clone
of myself
so that way

I could
kill myself,
but it just seems like
a lot of work.
Not to mention
my lab coat
is in the wash
and I'm out
of Cherry Coke Zero,
and I can't work
and be productive
and make a clone
of myself
without some Cherry Coke Zero,
    and besides,
I don't think I could make
a cloning machine
out of colored construction paper
and bendy straws
and glue
and Cheerios
and that's all I have
so that means I'd need to go out
and buy new supplies
and I don't really have
much money
either
to buy all those things
with.
Plus it's really cold out
and I don't feel like
moving away
from my heater.
That and the fact
that I can't even remember
the last place I saw
my cloning machine
blueprints
and the last thing
I wanna do

is get up and turn
the entire house
upside down
trying to find them
especially when
I didn't sleep well
last night
and now I'm all tired
and cranky
and anxious
because of it.
Nope.
That doesn't appeal
to me at all,
so right now
the easiest thing to do
is just sit here
in front of my computer
and catch up
on all of the old episodes
of *Ghost Hunters*
that I missed
while thinking about
how nice it'd be
if I had a clone
of myself
so that way
I could
kill myself.

I know
I'd never
kill myself
though.

Sometimes
it's just nice
to think
about.

The same way
it's fun to wonder
where this weird
#2 shaped
birthmark
on my arm
came from
because I don't ever
remember
having it
when I was little.

Today
I broke into tears
over an
Avril Lavigne
song
that came on
the radio.

Maybe
it's a good thing
I'm so
lazy.

ugly, black butterflies

I felt really alone
today.

I felt so alone
that I just sat
in my parked car
outside of Burger King
and watched the cars
drive past
in the street.
It was a real busy street
and the cars
went by really fast.
The cars went
vroom, Vroom, VROOM,
and as they whizzed by
they looked like small, speeding whales
made out of metal
and they looked inviting
and friendly
and their headlights
and front grills
looked like faces
with eyes
and smiles,
    and me,
I was jealous
of their smiles
because I was wearing
a frown
on my face.
I wore a great, big frown
on my face
as I sat there
all alone
in the Burger King
parking lot
watching the cars

whiz by.

I was frowning
because I was hiding
from my loneliness
back home.
I felt lonely there
in the parking lot too
but back home
it was much worse.
        Much, *much* worse.
I couldn't go back home
because if I did
my loneliness
would find me
and it'd wrap itself
around my head
like a koala bear
wrapping itself
around a tree
and when that happens
I really can't see clearly
with a face full
of koala cooter,
and if I don't see clearly
I don't think clearly,
and when I don't think clearly
I don't know what to do
with myself
and I feel sick
and I feel like
I wanna vomit up
all the ugly, black
butterflies I have
fluttering around
inside my tummy.

The cars
sure did look
friendly

as they raced past.
    Peaceful even.
They went
vroom, Vroom, VROOM,
and they called out to me
with their
vroom, Vroom, VROOMS,
so I got out of my car
and opened my trunk
and looked inside
but what I was hoping
to find in there
wasn't there.
What I was hoping
to find in my trunk
was a deer costume.
I don't know why
I kind of expected
to find one in there.
It's not like I've ever
driven around
while keeping a deer costume
in my trunk
but I guess I just figured,
    Hell,
weirder things
have happened.

I wanted there to be
a deer costume
in my trunk
so I could have
put it on
and then,
    with my deer costume on,
I would've had the courage
to blindly prance
back and forth
across the busy street
until one of the cars

eventually hit me
and splattered my guts
and innards
across the road
and set
all the ugly, black
butterflies I have
fluttering inside of tummy
free.
Then people wouldn't have thought
I was a coward
for killing myself.
They would've just thought
I was a stupid, startled
dumb-ass deer
and I'd rather die
being thought of as
a stupid, startled
dumb-ass deer
than as a coward,

although,

    to be honest,

I don't think people
who kill themselves
are cowards.

People who kill themselves
are sick.

    Not of the body,
but of the mind
and of the soul.

So if sick people
who kill themselves
are cowards
then so is every sick person

who's ever died of AIDS
or cancer.

I don't think either type
are cowards
though.
I just think
people get sick
and suffer
and die sometimes
because of it.

I'm sick.
That's why I have
ugly, black
butterflies
fluttering around
inside my tummy.

The second
you stop viewing life
as a gift
or as a journey
or as an experience
you're practically placing
a flaming bag of poo
on Lady Death's
doorstep.

I want all of these
ugly, black
butterflies
fluttering around
inside my tummy
to go away.

I need
to stop looking
at life
like it's a tangled
slinky.

death in between the B and N keys on my keyboard (all alone together)

I was sitting
in front of
my computer
and I had just finished
masturbating
and I was looking down
at my penis
        and as I was looking down
at my penis
my penis reminded me of
a balloon
after you let
all the air
out of it
and it *zooms,*
                zooms,
                        zooms
around the room
making loud farting noises
and then
it crash lands
and lies motionless
looking
all shriveled
and tired
and exhausted.

My dick looked like
a deflated balloon
and this didn't
make me happy.
        It made me sad.
It made me sad
because no guy
wants his dick
to look like a
shriveled,

tired,
exhausted,
deflated balloon,
but it really made me sad
because I was a
shriveled,
tired,
exhausted,
deflated balloon
too,

and I was shriveled
and tired
and exhausted
from a meaningless,
worthless
journey
full of farting noises.
A journey
I didn't wanna take.
A journey
I didn't ask for.
A journey
I didn't understand

and I had
run out of air
and I had
crash landed
somewhere
    and I was lost
too.

Not literally
though.

I wasn't literally
lost.

I knew

where I was.

I was
at home,
in my basement,
in my chair,
in front of my computer.

But I was
at home
and I knew
where I was
and yet
I still felt lost,
and I think
knowing where I was
and still feeling lost
was what made me feel
so lost,
so sad,
so alone.

Then,
as I was looking at
my shriveled,
tired,
exhausted
penis,
I felt something fall
on top of
my head
and it bounced off
my hair
and landed in between
the B and N keys
on my keyboard.

I looked down
at it
and it was

a spider.

A dead
spider.

A little,
itsy-bitsy,
shriveled-up,
dead spider.

I screamed
like a little girl
and jumped up
out of my chair
but don't get
the wrong idea.
I screamed
like a little girl
but in a very, very manly
way.

I screamed like
a little manly girl
and I looked down
at the spider
and the spider
was curled up
into a perfect ball.
He looked like
a tiny, black,
peaceful
beach ball.
I don't know how
beach balls
can look peaceful
but they just can
and he just did,

and I stood there
and I stared at him,

and as I stared at death
in between
the B and N keys
on my keyboard
I wondered how long
that spider
had been up there
just hanging out
above me.
I thought about
how he died
all alone
even though
he actually hadn't
because I was there
right beneath him
even though
I didn't know
he existed.

We were alone
together,
        he and I.

We were shriveled
and tired
and exhausted

and alone together
and I didn't even
know it
because I didn't know
that even when
you're looking at
your deflated
balloon-like penis,
        even when you think
you couldn't possibly be
more alone
in the world,
        you're not.

You are alone
but you're not,

and it makes
so much sense
that it almost
makes none
whatsoever

but when you
look at it
like that
your shriveled,
tired,
exhausted existence
doesn't hurt so bad
because we're all bonded
through our
loneliness
because we're all alone
together.

I left
the spider there,
put my dick
away
and went
upstairs.
Then
I got some
ice cream
out of the fridge
and began eating it.
It was
really good
ice cream
too.
I ate it
so fast
that I got brain freeze

but even though
I got brain freeze
I didn't stop
eating it,
    because
    like life,
death
is just so much easier
to face
when you have
ice cream.

Let the loneliness
sustain you
until love
finds a way
to.

the fighter

I had just finished
taking
this glorious,
monster poop
one afternoon
and as I was reaching
for a wad
of toilet paper
I realized
I still had a tiny
piece of poop
dangling
from my butthole.

I had a tiny
piece of poop
dangling
from my butthole
so I did
what most anyone
would do.
I shook
and shimmied
my ass around
trying to make
the piece of poop
fall off of me,
        but it didn't.

It didn't
fall off
of me
so I shook
a little more
and then a little more
but the stubborn
piece of poop
still wouldn't fall off

of my butthole.
It just
clung to me.
It clung
to my butthole
with this seemingly
unbreakable, kung fu-like
grip
and no matter
how hard
I shook
and shimmied my ass
the little
piece of poop
just wouldn't
let go
and fall into
the toilet.

So I kept shaking
and I kept shaking
and I shook
and shimmied my ass
so much
that I began to get
winded.

I couldn't
believe it.

Well,
        actually,
I couldn't believe
two things.

Firstly
I couldn't believe
that I was in
such bad shape
that I could get winded

from simply
trying to shake
poop
off of my asshole,
and secondly
I couldn't
believe
that after all
that shaking
that the piece of poo
was still
hanging on to
me.

He was still
hanging
on to me,

and as I sat there
panting
and trying to catch
my breath
I suddenly
pictured that
"Hang in there!" poster
of the cat
from back in the 70s,
and as soon
as I pictured that
"Hang in there!" poster
of the cat
from back in the 70s
everything changed.

Everything changed
because I didn't want
the piece of poop
to fall off
of my butthole
and into the toilet

anymore.

He was just trying
to hang in there
and I
was just trying
to hang in there
too.
I was just trying
to hang in there
in a world
that was relentlessly
shaking
and shimmying
its asshole
and trying to make me
fall off
and then
inside my head
I was like,
Oh my, God!
Don't let go!
Hang in there,
little buddy!

I don't know
why I called

my dingleberry
"little buddy."
I don't know
why I talked
to my dingleberry
inside my head
like I was The Skipper
and he was Gilligan
but I did.

I just did.

I just did

because all
he and I
both wanted
was a fair shot.

A fair shot
without having
too much
thrown at us
and too much
stolen away
from us.

So I did
what any good person
who has poo
dangling from
their butthole
should do.

I sat there
for three
hours.

I sat there
for three
hours
until I heard
the softest
and most solemn of
    KER-PLUNKs!
I had ever heard
in my entire
life.

I stood up
and I looked
at him there
underwater,
    the brave

little guy
that he was,
and even though
he was brown,
  and even though
he was only the size
of my pinky's fingernail,
he looked like
Mark Wahlberg
from that movie,
The Fighter,

and as I stood there
staring at him
I heard "Taps"
playing
in my head.
I heard "Taps"
playing
in my head
so I saluted him
and I'd be lying
if I said
that I didn't get
  at least
a little bit misty-eyed
over it all,
  because I did,
and I wanted
so badly
to pin
a medal on him.
A medal
for his valor
and courage
but I didn't
because I didn't have
a medal on me
because it's not like
I walk around

carrying medals
on me
or anything.
Plus
I didn't wanna
touch my poo
either.

That'd be
gross.

    Life
is gross.

Life
is a gross, ugly
asshole
we're all trying
to hang on to
even though
a lot of the time
we're not
even sure
why.

We all
eventually
let go
and fall
but it's
the hanging on
that matters
because it's
the hanging on
that gets remembered.

People
don't remember
Hemingway
for blowing

his brains out
with a shotgun.

If they do
they probably
just don't get it
anyway.

I don't think
I'll kill myself
today.

Who knew that
poo
could be
inspirational?

real happiness not included, stupid

I was particularly
unhappy
one day
so I went to McDonald's
and got myself
a Happy Meal
to make myself
feel better.
I got myself
a Happy Meal
because Happy Meals
always used to
make me feel happy
when I was little.

So I got my Happy Meal
and I sat down
and I opened it up
and I pulled out
the toy.
It was a car,
        a race car to be exact.
The race car
was the boy toy,
and I got the boy toy
because I was a boy,
and I looked at
the race car
and I thought,
        Oooooooh ...
                pretty cool.
And then I put it down
and began nibbling
on my fries
because when I was little
and my parents bought me
a Happy Meal
the rule was

I couldn't play with the toy
until after I had eaten
all of my food
but then I was like,
    Fuck it ...
I'm a grown-ass man
and I paid for this Happy Meal
with my own
grown-ass money,
so I ripped open
the little plastic bag
and took the race car out
and began racing it
across the table
and it went,
    VROOOOM! VROOOOOM!
Eeeeeeeeeeerttttttt!
        CRASHHHHH!
and I played with
the race car
for awhile.
I played with
the race car
for awhile
but then I began to feel
naughty
as I played with it
    but not the good kind of naughty
like when you spank
a woman's ass
in bed.
I felt the guilty
kind of naughty
like I was betraying my parents
for playing with the toy
when I should've been eating
and I could see them
shaking their heads at me
in disappointment
inside my head.

Then I was like,
    Okay, okay.
I'll eat my food ...

So I put my boy toy
race car away
and I began eating
my food
but it was all cold
and gross,
    and don't get me wrong,
that didn't stop me
from devouring it
almost instantly
because I'm so
incurably chubby,
but I just didn't enjoy
my food that much
and so I sat there
with a stupid race car
boy toy
which was no fun
anymore
and with an aching tummy
full of greasy, cold food
and I thought
to myself,
    Man,
        what a ripoff!!!
There should be
a disclaimer
on the box
for stupid people like me.
A disclaimer
that says,
"Real happiness
not included."

So I just sat there
in my booth

and I was real bummed,
and there was this
really doofy-looking guy
in ugly-ass plaid shorts
sitting in the same side
of the booth
as his really cute girlfriend,
and all I could think
as I looked at them
was,
        Man,
I need to get me
some plaid shorts,

and then
I was even more bummed
because all I could think about was
how all my friends
were growing up
and were getting engaged
        or were already married,
and how they were all having kids
and starting families
and buying houses
and I was a 27-year-old
buying Happy Meals,
        taking blind stabs
at happiness
in the dark
because that was all
I could afford
to do,

and they all drove
brand new cars,
        my grown-up friends
                that is,
and I had a boy toy
race car
that went,

VROOOOM! VROOOOOM!
Eeeeeeeeeeeerttttttt!
CRASHHHHH!
when you played
with it,
and I wanted that cute girl
in the booth
across from me
and I wanted all those
other things
too.
I wanted them
real bad
and they all seemed
so untouchable,
so impossible,
and then I thought to myself
about how much
this life
eats away at you,
about how much
it demands
and takes away
from you
and how much
it hurts
and how it will never
stop hurting
no matter how good
it gets
either,
and then
I felt like
a dumb, little kid
for making such
a dumb,
childish
decision,

and then

I looked down at my boy toy
race car
and I heard it going,
    VROOOOM! VROOOOOM!
Eeeeeeeeeeeerttttttt!
        CRASHHHHH!
and then this voice
inside my head
told me
a secret.
It sounded old
and wise
and black.
It sounded
like Morgan Freeman,
and Morgan Freeman's voice
whispered
to me,
    There is nothing
childish
or immature
about licking your lips
and hiking up your pants
and chasing after the gods
with nothing but clenched fists,
and doing so takes
just as much courage,
    if not more so,
than to be
one of the faceless heroes
who slave away
after salvation
chiseling away
at their own epitaphs.

Then I felt
a little bit better.

I felt
a little bit better

because even though
there was a really good chance
that someday
I'd be a lonely,
penniless,
70-year-old man
buying himself Happy Meals
and playing with boy toy
race cars,
	there was hope; hope
that by following
these silly,
childish
dreams
that somehow
I'd maybe get lucky
and through their pursuit
I'd become
half the man
my father is,

	and if I got *really* lucky
maybe I'd even
catch myself
a god.
I'd catch him
by the seat of his pants
and then I'd force him
to sit down with me
and have a drink
and we would
raise our glasses
and toast to ourselves,
	to ourselves
and no one else …

But that's a long way
away
and I won't be
wearing plaid shorts

if all that does happen
because I think
plaid shorts
are ugly,
and until that
glorious moment arrives
all I have to remember
is one thing
and one thing
only …

Food first.

Then toy.

VROOOOM! VROOOOOM!
Eeeeeeeeeeeerttttttt!
CRASHHHHH!

CHAPTER TWO

the nipples taste like nipples! the snozberries taste like snozberries!

Last night
you were naked
and then
you fell asleep
in my arms.

As you tossed
and turned slightly
in your sleep
one of your boobs
popped out
from underneath
the covers.
I noticed it
immediately
and I
stared at it
and I
stared at it.

I wanted
to lick it.

    Especially
your nipple.

I wanted
to lick
your nipple
very, very gently
like I was a kitten
licking milk
from a saucer.
Then I found myself
wanting to lick
your nipple
nice and hard

and over
and over
and over again
too
as if it were
lickable wallpaper,
like the kind
Willy Wonka has
inside his chocolate factory.
I wanted to lick
your nipple
over
and over
because I think your nipples
taste amazing.
    In fact,
I think
your nipples taste
even better
than snozberries.
Yep,
    I said it.
And I stand by it
too.
Your nipples taste
even better
than snozberries.

And as I just lay there
staring at your tasty boob
with its tasty nipple
that tastes
even better
than snozberries
I realized your boob
was staring back
at me.
We were having
a staring contest,
    the two of us,

but I'm horrible
at staring contests
and I blinked
and I lost
and then
I smiled.

Ohhh, boob.
    You devil, you …
    You win.
    You always do.

Then
I found myself
wanting to grab it.
Christ,
how I wanted to
grab it.
I wanted to grab it
and squeeze it
and lick it
sooo bad
but I couldn't
bring myself
to do it.
I couldn't
bring myself
to grab
and squeeze
and lick
your boob
because I was afraid
I'd wake you up
and I didn't wanna
wake you up.
You looked
so cute
as you lay
asleep
on my arm,

divine
even,
and you were
drooling on my arm
just a little bit too
but that only made you
even more cute.
Most guys
probably wouldn't like
being drooled on
by a girl
but I didn't mind
you drooling
on me
at all.
Actually,
I liked it.
You looked
like an angel.
Like a cute,
adorable,
drooling
angel
with really nice boobs.
Then I remembered
your boob
out there
in the open
and I looked
at it
again.

"Wow ..."
I said aloud.

I couldn't believe it.

When
I was younger,
and much chubbier,

I never thought
in a million years
that I'd ever
get to
see a boob
in real life
let alone
lick one
or
squeeze one
and pretty much
whenever
I wanted to
too,

and then
while looking
at your boob
I remembered
that I can have
ice cream
for breakfast
and a Capri Sun
for lunch
and cookies
for dinner
and that the world
can be
beautiful
if you want it to.
If you want to
see it that way
the world
can be
so,
  so,
    childishly beautiful,

and at that moment
the world *was*

beautiful
and your boob
was beautiful
and it was magical
too,
and I would've bet anything
that at that very moment
your boob could've pulled
a rabbit
out of a hat
or a quarter
out of my ear.

I turned
and looked at
your face.
Your face
was beautiful too.
You were
still drooling on me
and it was cute
and it was warm
and it was love,
so I leaned over
and licked the drool
off of your chin
and then I kissed
your earlobe
simply because
it was there.
Then
I closed my eyes
and tried
to fall
asleep.

I had cheated
life
enough
for

one
night.

milking a dead cow

I hope she doesn't
call me tonight.

I love hearing from her
and
I love hearing her voice
but whenever she calls
I never have
anything to say.

I'm afraid
she's going to
catch on.
I'm afraid
the silence
is going to
rat me out.
Sooner or later
she's going to
discover
that there's nothing
there,
that there's nothing
inside of me.

Yesterday
I farted
and a moth
came out …

I caught him
and ripped off
his wings
and crammed him
back up inside
my ass,
 the little bastard …
He won't be

trying that again
anytime soon.

If she calls me
tonight
I'll just lie.
I'll tell her
that she caught me
at a bad time,
that I'm busy
practicing my dropkicks
for the big, annual
dropkicking contest
coming up
this weekend,
that I really need to
buckle down
and practice my dropkicks
if I wanna get
the blue ribbon
this year
and keep that asshole
Bill Dwyer
from winning it
again.

Then before she can offer
to come and watch me
and be there for moral support
    (and she would too
    because she's really
    fucking sweet like that),
I'll smash my phone
on to the ground.

That will buy me
at least
a couple days.
That will give me
a little time

to figure something
out
because although
she doesn't know it
yet

she's beating
an empty piñata,

she's milking
a dead cow.

She's a good one
                        too,
                              this girl,
and she deserves
so much more
than these empty promises
of candy
and milk
that I've made
to her.

I need to figure
something out.

I dunno …

Maybe it'll
help me think
if I get back to
practicing
my dropkicks …

… Fuckin' Bill Dwyer.

goodbye, smiles

She
doesn't smile at me
anymore
after I kiss her.
She
used to smile at me
all the time
after I kissed her,
a great big grin
from ear to ear,
and I'd think,
    Man,
what a great kisser
I am.
I must really be
the best.
But I can't take all the credit.
Good job, lips.
    Good work, tongue.
        You guys make a great team!

I loved seeing
her smile at me
after we kissed.
She would smile at me
so big
and so wide
that I thought the corners
of her lips
were going to tear
and rip into her cheeks
and blood was going to spurt out
everywhere
and all over my face.
That would've been really gross.
Plus I don't do well
with blood.
Seeing a lot of it

makes me want to pass out
like I have
the vapors
or something.
So I'm glad I never saw
her smile
tear into her cheeks
like that,
    but at the same time
        if it ever had happened,
I secretly would've been
at least
a little bit happy
knowing that it was
because of me
that she had torn her face
smiling.

But
I don't have to worry
about that happening
anymore
because she
no longer smiles at me
after I kiss her.
I don't know why.
I really wonder
what it could be.
I don't have bad breath.
I don't eat stinky foods
like onions
or garlic
or Limburger cheese.
I brush my teeth
too.
I also floss.
    Well,
not every day.
Occasionally though,
and I chew minty gum

too,
    and I shower.
I think I smell good,
so I don't know what it is.

Maybe I'm just not good
at kissing anymore.
Maybe I'm slipping.
Maybe I just need
to practice
my kissing a little bit.
I could do that.
I could practice
my kissing.
Look ...
Mwah!
    Mwah!
        Mwah!!!
There.
I feel like a better kisser
already.
I hope that's all it is.

The one before her
stopped smiling
after I kissed her
too
and then she left me
but I guess that's what happens
sometimes.
Women leave you
and they take away
the kisses,
and the head
and the hand jobs
and the fucking
but what always comes closest
to killing me
is that they take away
the smiles

too.

The smiles
are always
the first to go,
and then, all at once,
they suddenly take away
the smell of their hair,
their laughter,
the after-sex showers,
the kitten noises
they make
as they become sleepy,
the sitcom lullabies,
the sighs of euphoria
they let out
as they lay down in your arms
because you make them
feel safe, and,
in return,
you feel more like
a man
than you ever have
in your entire
life.
They take away
all those things,
all those wonderful things
which returned levity
to your encumbered
being.

Amy,
you have already taken away
the smiles.
When you take away
everything else
please
do it slowly
and steadily.

It may be long
and painful
but this way
it will not
kill me.
You see,
        Amy,
I can get kisses
from any girl,
from any person,
even from your roommate's dog.
        He tries to kiss me
                all the time.
But what I can't get
from any of them
is your smile.
So please,
either give it back
or let me go.

        I think
that's right.

        I think
that's only
fair.

you're sure you still don't wanna shower with me?

Now
that you're gone
I need to learn
how to be
alone
again.

I have to
relearn
how to sleep alone,
how to eat alone,
how to watch movies alone,
how to take showers alone,
    and let me tell you,
showers
just aren't as fun
without a nice, cute,
naked girl
showering
next to you.

I took
a shower
yesterday
alone
and it made me
sad.
It made me sad
because you weren't there
naked,
singing
and dancing
and wiggling your wet butt
to punk rock tunes
playing on
your phone.
When the shower head

saw you weren't there
with me today
it cried salty tears
on me
instead of water
and that made me
wanna cry too
because crying
can be contagious
like laughing,
and like herpes,
and like laughing herpes.
I was so sad
I didn't know
what to do
so I just stood there
and thought about how
if you hold
a black comb facing
downwards
on your upper lip
it looks like a mustache
but if you hold it
facing upwards
over your lips
it looks like you have
a robot smile.
Those are
the kinds of things
you think about
when you're sad
and alone
and the shower head
is crying
on you.

Then I remembered
I was supposed to be
showering
but I didn't wanna

shower alone
so I went to my room
and grabbed my old, stuffed
teddy bear.
His name
is Cool Bear.
I've had him
since I was six months old
and he and I
used to be pretty tight
so I had him
shower with me.
It wasn't the same
as when you showered
with me
though.
He didn't sing
or dance
or wiggle his wet butt.
    Actually,
it was kind of awkward.
He just stared at me
the whole time
with this really blank
expression
on his face.
It made me
uncomfortable,
    really uncomfortable,
so I tried
washing his back
like I used to
wash yours
but it wasn't
nearly
as nice.
You had nice, clean,
smooth skin
and he had fur.
Lathering up

a furry back
doesn't feel nice.
        Not even a little bit.
Actually it feels
kind of gross.
My dick used to get hard
lathering up your back
but I didn't even
come close
to getting hard
lathering up his back.
I don't think stuffed animals
are meant to be
showered with
but I just didn't know
what else
to do.

The whole thing
was a bad idea.
If anything
it just made me
miss you more,
        and although
I wasn't aware of it
at the time,
it made me realize
I was beginning
to fall in love
with you
too.

Love
is having someone
who makes all the
mundane, boring shit
you have to do
on a daily basis
tolerable,
if not fun

and special.

Everything
felt much more special
with you around.
        Even just
sitting next to you
and biting my nails.

You're way better
than a teddy bear,
        and not to belittle Cool Bear,
but you give
way better head
too.

I miss you.

dinbu (boogie man food)

Sometimes
during the night
I startle myself
awake
from a bad dream
and I go
to reach for you
so I can hold on to you
and snuggle you
and cuddle you
and make myself
feel better,
      so
I reach over
towards your spot
and you won't
be there
      and I panic,
and the first conclusion
I always jump to
within a fraction
of a second
is that the boogie man
got you
and then
I really panic
and lose my shit
because once
the boogie man
gets you
you're as good
as dead.
      The boogie man
doesn't fuck around.
            Trust me ...
               I've heard some shit
               about the boogie man ...

But right before
I leap out of bed
and begin looking
for my baseball bat
to charge into battle
with
I remember
that you're gone
and that you're not there
and that you haven't been there
for almost three
years now,
and even though
you haven't been there
for almost three
years now
there's still
a small,
nagging
part of me
that suspects
I've woken up
in some bizarro world
where cats and dogs
get along
and where people pee
out of their fingers
and where
you and I
are no longer
together
and where
I have to pick
the lint
out of my own
bellybutton.

That was
your job.

Do you remember
doing that?

You used to
put a quarter in my mouth
and I'd swallow it down
into my tummy
and then you'd
twist my left ear
and a piece of lint
would roll out
into my bellybutton
and then you'd
take it out
like it was a gumball.
At least
that's the way
I remember it.
I may
or may not have
taken some artistic liberties
there
but that's the way
I remember it,
and you'd take
the piece of lint
out of my bellybutton
like it was
a gumball
but you wouldn't
chew it.
You'd never
chew it
because you were smart
and you knew lint
wasn't for chewing.
You'd just throw it
somewhere on the bed
instead of in the garbage
and then you'd smile at me

and my soul
would melt
like an ice cream cone
in a microwave
and I'd think,

I can't wait
until I get to
watch her
pick the lint
out of our kids'
bellybuttons.
She's really good
at it.
She's the best
bellybutton lint picker
I've ever seen.
Why she could go
all-state
with those kinda
bellybutton lint picking skills
that she has.
Our kids are probably
going to
go to school
and be all like,
"My dad
can beat up
your dad
and my mom
can pick bellybutton lint
out of bellybuttons
better than
your mom can!"
and they'd be right
too,
at least
about the mom part.

Those nights

when I wake up
and panic
because I think
you've become
boogie man food,
        those nights
are murderous nights
        (almost as murderous
        as if the boogie man
        were to get his hands
        on me)
because
on those nights
I'm too tired
to pretend
that you
crossing me out
like a spelling error
almost three years ago
doesn't still hurt,

that
your bright smile
shining at me
from the shadows
of the past
with its goring,
                goring
                        persistence
doesn't still hurt,

and what almost
murders me
every night
is I know
that lost love,
        good or bad,
cannot be
forgotten.
It can only

be lived with
like a runny nose,
like a gimp leg,
like a gassy aunt,
like a cat who just can't learn
to poo inside
the litter box.

No one
will ever call you
Dinbu
ever again.

Does that
make you sad?

    Probably not …

I wish
the boogie man
really had
eaten you.

going to a water park is more fun than returning an engagement ring

You know
what's fun?
    Going to
a water park.

You know
what's not fun?
    Returning
an engagement
ring.

If you ever
get the choice
of getting to go
to a water park
or
having to return
an engagement ring
I highly
recommend
you choose
going to
a water park.

Water parks
are fun.

They have
wave pools
and water slides
and lazy rivers
and concession stands
full of drinks
and snacks
and treats,
and they have cute girls
in itsy-bitsy bikinis

diving into water
and getting all wet
and shit,
and the girls
even come down
those long slides
and at the end
they stand up
and they have
a huge wedgie
and it looks like
they're wearing a thong
and then
you get to watch them
as they pick
their bathing suits
from out of
their asses
        and it's really
pretty fuckin'
awesome.

Returning
an engagement
ring
involves
none of
those things.
Returning
an engagement
ring
wouldn't be so bad
if it
at least
somehow involved
cute, wet girls
picking their bathing suit
wedgies,
but returning
an engagement

ring
involves
nothing like that
whatsoever.

Returning
an engagement
ring
involves
watching
an extremely
flamboyant
and kind-hearted
jeweler
walk away
holding
a tiny,
velvet box,
and watching
the jeweler
walk away
with that tiny,
velvet box
is like watching
a nurse
walk away
with the cold,
lifeless body
of the beautiful
baby girl
you and your girlfriend
were supposed
to have together,
        but instead
your beautiful
baby girl
died,
and she died
even before
she ever had a chance

to breathe,
even before
you ever had the chance
to see her
smile,
and as the jeweler
walks away
with the tiny,
velvet box,
it no longer
looks like
a tiny,
velvet box.
It looks like
a tiny,
velvet coffin,
and you
get to watch
the jeweler
take your baby girl
away from you
in that tiny,
velvet coffin
and then
you just stand there.
And
you stand there
all alone
too.

Well,
not *all*
alone.

You stand there
and you stare at
the hundreds
of rings
in their glass cases
and they stare back

at you
and keep you
company
while they dance
beneath their lights
in a sparkling ballet
of your failure
and loss.

When
you go to
the water park
and you
need to pee
you can just go
right there
in the water
and it's
absolutely
amazing.

When
the jeweler
walked away
with the ring
I peed myself
right there

in the store
but it wasn't
the same
as in the water park.
It wasn't
amazing
at all.

Yeah …

Going to
a water park
is *definitely*

more fun
than returning
an engagement
ring.

every time i see my cat's balls i think of you

He's my cat
now,
but *my* cat
used to be
our cat,
but then you left
making *our* cat
simply
my cat,

and every time
I see *my* cat's balls
I think of you.

I'll be doing whatever
and I'll notice
his balls
and his cute, little,
orange,
fuzzy balls
will suddenly transform
into dancing mirages
of your smiling,
pretty face
and I'll think about that time
we were living together
and you were sitting
on the floor
and you were on
your laptop
and he was standing
in front of you
with his tail up
and his balls out
and you noticed his balls
and you just sat there
and stared at them.

You stared
and stared
and stared,
and as you stared
at his balls
I could see
your entire world
disappear
around you,
    and then,
        with the most
        child-like curiosity,
you reached over
and ever so gently
poked
one of his furry balls
with the tip
of your pointer finger
and then he freaked out
and ran away
into the other room.

You looked over
and saw me
and realized that
I had caught you
poking our cat's balls.
You didn't know
what else to do
so you smiled at me,
and you smiled at me
the same way
a little girl
who had just been caught
drawing on the walls
with crayons
would smile
at her father,
    and I never really
wanted kids,

but at that moment
I could feel the weight
of an invisible,
beautiful,
baby girl
in my arms,

the beautiful
baby girl
I never knew I wanted
until I saw you poke
our cat's balls,

until I found something
so special
and so wondrous
in another human being
that it made me
want to create life
just to make sure
all those special,
wondrous qualities
got passed on
into the future world.

Then
you left me.

You left me
and you made
our cat
    my cat,
and every time
I see my cat's balls
I think of you.

I know
I should get him
neutered
but I can't

bring myself
to have it done.

Maybe
I'm waiting
for another girl
to come along
and poke
my cat's balls
and that's how
I'll know
she's the one.
Almost like a
    The Sword in the Stone
    type-thing
but with fingers
and cat balls
instead.

I know
that will never
happen
though
and that's why
losing you
still hurts
so bad.

That's why
I can still
feel the weight
of our invisible,
beautiful,
baby girl
in my arms.

I wish
you could
see her.

She smiles
just like
you.

sometimes i miss you all the time

Sometimes
I miss you
all the time.

Sometimes
I hate you
all the time
too
though.

    I dunno …
        Don't ask me.
            It's *really* confusing,
kind of like
basic algebra.

Even though
sometimes
I miss you
all the time
and even though
sometimes
I hate you
all the time
every now and then
I'll still secretly
masturbate to you,
    but shhhhh,
        don't tell anyone;
        it's a secret.

I tell the walls
to close their eyes
and then,
    when I'm sure
    those perverted shits
    aren't peeking,
I'll masturbate

to memories
of you and I fucking
and I'm pretty sure
that masturbating
to memories
makes me
the most pathetic person
alive,
    but even so,
that hasn't stopped me
from doing it
or anything.

Most of the time
when I do masturbate
to memories
of you and I fucking
I masturbate
to that time
when you took me
to your family reunion
up in some cabin
deep in the woods
and I met your family,
    and your whole
    extended family
    too,
and there were so many people
around us all the time
that we had to sneak out
into the woods
just to have sex
and so we snuck out
and we fucked
right next to some queer,
old-ass, ramshackle
shed
and then I pulled out
and came all over
your ass.

We had
nothing else to use
to clean your ass off
with
so I wiped my cum
off your ass
with some dead leaves
that I picked up
off the ground,
and for some weird reason
as I wiped my cum
off your butt
I felt like I was back
in art class
in grade school.
I felt
like I was working on
the greatest art assignment
ever,
and as I wiped off
your ass
I told myself,
You'll never
forget this moment
for as long
as you live,
and as I stood there
wiping my cum
off your ass
I felt myself
turning into Michelangelo.
Not the Ninja Turtle
though.
The painter,

and every dab
and every wipe
was like a soft brush stroke
full of love
and purpose

because I was
the first and last man
who would ever
wipe cum
off your ass
with a leaf.
I was capturing
a moment,
    a wondrous,
        brilliant moment,

one that seemed
to connect us
and bring us even closer
than the sex
we just had,

and I was so proud
of the art
I was creating
that a part of me
wanted to take home
one of the leaves
that I had used
and hang it on
my family's fridge
with a magnet
and then I wanted to light it
with a spotlight
and section it off
by putting it behind
a velvet rope.
    I wanted to do that
but I didn't.
I didn't
because spotlights
and velvet ropes
are pretty expensive
and I don't have
that kind of money.

I don't have
spotlight and velvet rope
money.
        Not even close …

When I was done
cleaning off your ass
we went back
to your family's cabin.
I took one look
at your gruff,
grouchy,
dick-headed
hick of a dad
and all of a sudden
he didn't intimidate me
anymore.
He didn't intimidate me
anymore
because I was a brilliant artist
and he was just
some old, crusty, rube
and then I did nothing
but smile
the rest of
our stay.

I masturbate
to that memory
every now and then
and after I've finished
my dick
is always pooped
and panting
and my balls
are tired
and empty
and I always have the urge
to clean myself up
with some leaves

but I don't have
any trees in my room
because trees grow outside
so I always end up
just having to use
a tissue
instead.
Then one of my cats
hops up
onto the bed
and tries to sniff the tissue
full of
sticky,
white
memories
that I'll never forget,
that I'll never get rid of
no matter how many times
I shoot them
out of my wiener.

I never thought
a crumpled up tissue
full of sperm
could look like
two turtle doves
kissing
but if you look at it
in just the right light
it does.

It really,
        sincerely
                does.

Sometimes
I miss you
all the time,

but not

right now.

Right now
I hate you
because to
    you
a crumpled up tissue
full of sperm
just looks like
a crumpled up tissue
full of sperm.

The next time
I've finished masturbating
to that memory
of you and I fucking
in the woods
I'm going to
climb onto my roof
and throw
the crumpled up tissue
full of sperm
into the air
and hope
and pray
that it splits into
two turtle doves
who fly away
in separate
directions.

Other than that
I have no idea
how
to stop
hating
you,

or loving you
for that

matter.

when the dawn comes, tonight will be a chubby memory too

Every once
in awhile
while digging around
inside my wallet,
or my coat pocket,
or pants pocket,
I'll come across
an old,
crumpled up,
wrinkled
receipt,
    and because
I'm such
an incurable fat ass
nine times
out of ten
the receipt
will be for one of many
fast food places:
    Taco Bell,
    Wendy's,
    McDonald's,
    Burger King,
        you know,
        the usuals,
and I'll look down
at the receipt
in my hand
and reread
what I had ordered
for lunch
or dinner
on that day …

4 SOFT TACO BEEF
    – NO LETTUCE

1 LRG DIET PEPSI

and if I'm lucky
the receipt will still have
some kind of grease stain
on it
and after I've made sure
no one is looking
I'll bring the receipt
up to my nose
and take a sniff
and breathe it in
and all the wonderfully
tasty
memories
will come flooding back
into my brain,

and as I reminisce
I'll smile,

and I'll feel warm
and good inside
and the sun
will suddenly piss
special
rays of sunshine
down upon me,
        and only
upon me,
and as the world dissolves
around me
I'll just stand there
wherever I may be
in a state of
chubby blissfulness
staring at the receipt
ever so longingly
almost as if it were
a photograph

of an old girlfriend
I had never really
gotten over
or a photo
of me and a bunch
of forgotten friends
that I dearly miss
and haven't seen in years
and know
I'll most likely
never see again,

and then
it will hurt,

because those tacos
were good tacos,
    really … good … tacos.

I remember them
so clearly,
so perfectly,
and I loved them
so much
and they tasted
so delicious
but I know they're
never
coming
back.

Those tacos,
those really, really good tacos
are gone.

The song
"Memory"
from Andrew Lloyd Webber's
Cats
will begin playing inside my head

and I'll become
misty-eyed
over the whole damn thing
and to keep from bawling
I'll have to
secretly scold myself …

Really, Calvero?
Really?
You're going to weep
in public
over an old
fast food receipt?
You pathetic,
sentimental
sack of shit!
You sniveling bitch …
There are plenty of tacos
in the sea.
Find your damn balls
and move on
with your life!

So I'll reach my hand
down into my pants,
wherever I may be,
and find my testicles
smushed inside
my boxers
(that's usually
where I find them
whenever I misplace them),
and with my balls
in hand
I'll finally snap out of it
and end up
throwing the receipt away
because a mind
that reminisces too often
is a mind

that murders the present
and smogs the future.

So with the receipt
in the trash
I'll just get in my car,
drive to the nearest Taco Bell
    (or other
    nearest fast food location),
and make some
brand new, tasty,
fat-ass
memories
to last me awhile,

    or at the very least

to last me
just long enough.

CHAPTER THREE

and purr
and brush up against her
and have her choose
  me
and have her take
  me
home with her.
Then at night
I would curl up
down at the end
of her bed
by her bare feet
as she read a book
before going to sleep,
and, knowing her,
  her toenails
would be painted
a really cute color,
like a light blue,
  or a fun surf green,
    or a teal,
and then,
  before turning off
the lights,
she'd put down her book
and sit up and lean over
and pet me lovingly
for a few minutes.
I'd purr
gratefully
and I'd lick her toes
as a thank you
because I'd be
a very grateful,
gracious
cat,
and then
we'd both go to sleep,
  content
    and happy

because
we loved one another,
and our love
for one another
would be pure
and simple
and effortless,
and it'd be pure
and simple
and effortless
because she'd be thinking
I was a cat

because love
is never pure
and simple
and effortless
between
human beings.

Between
human beings
love
is a lie
with an expiration date,

and because of this
I'm pretty sure
the only way
to get another
human being
to love you
fully
and wholly
and unconditionally
is by pretending
to be a cat
and by sleeping
by their feet
and licking their toes,

because people
know how to love animals
but people
don't know how to love
other people,
    at least not
properly,
    at least not
in the ways
they should.

Then,
    after my pretty
Bond girl
in a ponytail
had fallen asleep,
I'd sneak up
over by her head
and in a whisper
I'd sing to her.

    I'd sing,

"Everyday,
it's a-gettin' closer.
Goin' faster
than a roller coaster.
Love like yours will
surely come my way.
A-hey,
    a-hey-hey ..."

and then
I'd curl up
by her feet
and fall asleep
happy
and content
and so full of life
and love

that I'd never ask
for anything more
than I already had,

that I'd never ask
for anything more
than my pretty girl
and her bare feet.

"*A-hey,*
a-hey-hey …"

cinnabons don't grow on trees

I just locked eyes
with this pretty blonde girl
who has her hair
up in a bun
and when we locked eyes
I got embarrassed
and turned away.
I got embarrassed
because I'm pretty sure
she was able
to read my mind
when we locked eyes,
    and when we locked eyes
I was thinking about
how cute she was
and that I liked
her nose
and that I wanted
to grab it
and pretend
to steal it from her
like you would
with a baby
and then be like,
    "Got your nose!!!"

I'm so embarrassed
now.
I know
she's a mind reader.
I know
she knows
that I wanna
grab her nose
and pretend
to steal it from her
because I think
it's cute.

I wonder
if I'm blushing …
        I bet I am.
                I *know* I am.

I'm gonna
smash my face
on the table
over and over
until it's beaten red
and bloody
so that way at least
it won't look like
I'm blushing
over her.

She looks tasty
                too,
        this blonde girl.

She sure
makes me hungry.
Not that
I'm a cannibal
or anything.
It's just that
her hair being up
in a bun
reminds me
of a Cinnabon
and it looks like
she has a Cinnabon
on top of her head
made of her hair.
        She's cute
and I wanna nibble
on her cute nose
and her Cinnabon
hair bun
like a field mouse.

She makes me hungry
even though I just had
a double quarter pounder
with cheese
and a large fry
for lunch.

Christ,
why am I
such a fat ass?

I'd give anything
to be able to
nibble
on her nose
and her Cinnabon
hair bun
while making love
to her
with my penis.

It's winter
outside
and the trees
look like dead roots
reaching up to the sky
for nourishment
and num nums,
but even though
they look dead
there's love
hiding
inside those trees.
        I *know* there is …

I'm going to do
ten push-ups
real quick
and then I'll be totally ripped
and I'll be able ask out

the cute blonde girl
and then I'll be able
to nibble
on her nose
and her Cinnabon
hair bun.

Okay,
push-ups!

Here we go!

One!
    Two!
        Three …
            Four …………………

Okay,
Four is good enough!
    Whew!

That was a
bad idea …
Now I'm all winded
and sweaty
and gross.

It doesn't matter
though.
    She's gone.
Cute, blonde girl left
without saying
goodbye,
without giving me
so much as
a look.
Now I'm sad
and still hungry
and wet
and gross

and I kinda feel like how
a mop must feel
after it mops
the floor.

Valentine's Day
is a week
from today.
I'm going to have
Cinnabon
for breakfast,
lunch,
and dinner
that day.

Loneliness
is so much easier
with Cinnabons.

Loneliness
is so much easier
when the trees
aren't being
a bunch
of stingy,
leafless
assholes.

would you be my corn muffin?

I was sitting
on the train
and I had just finished
a corn muffin
    and it was a really tasty
corn muffin
too,
    and because
I'm so innately chubby,
I sat there
on the train
all by myself
and all I could think about
was how much
I really missed
the tasty corn muffin
I had just
devoured.

I missed
my corn muffin
a lot.

    So much so
that I just sat there
in my seat
and stared longingly
at the numerous
corn muffin crumbs
that had fallen
on my crotch
wishing they could somehow
collect themselves
and gel together
like the T-1000
from *Terminator 2*
and form a new,
smaller corn muffin

for me to eat
and enjoy,

and the thought of that
made me real happy
at first,
but then the thought of that
made me real sad
at second.

It made me real sad
because I was missing
a corn muffin.

    Not
a person.
    A corn muffin …

I was missing
a corn muffin
and missing
a corn muffin
is sad,

and sometimes
I feel like
I'm missing people
but when I do
I'm never sure
who it is
I'm missing,
and when you're not sure
who it is
you're missing
I'm pretty sure
that just means
you miss
having people
to miss,

and as I sat there
missing
my corn muffin
I felt the train
come to a stop.
I felt the train
come to a stop
so I made myself
stop staring at my crotch
because
I didn't want the people
getting on
to walk by
and be like,
    Yo,
what's with this lunatic
who can't stop
staring
at his crotch?

and it was
a good thing
I did make myself stop
staring at my crotch
because as I looked up
this red-headed girl
walked over
and sat down
in the seat
in front of me
and she was
really pretty
    this red-headed girl,
and as I looked
at her
I could feel it.
    I could feel her
giving my heart
a boner.

I could feel
my heart
getting horny
for her heart
because she was
really pretty
and because
she was wearing
an olive-colored
pea coat
which I thought was
so cute
and so funny
for some reason,
and even though
I didn't know her
at all
I was like,
Oh
that's soooo
something
she would do.
That's soooo
like her
to wear an ***olive****-colored*
pea *coat,*

and I secretly giggled
to myself
at what a character
she was,
and as she fidgeted around
trying to get comfortable
in her seat
in front of me
I looked at the beautiful back
of her beautiful head
and her hair
was a little bit damp
and her damp hair

led me
to hypothesize
that she had either
just been snorkeling
        or
that she had just recently
taken a shower
and I ended up guessing
that she had just recently
taken a shower
because she smelled good
and because
not too many people
go snorkeling
in New England
either.
        Especially not
during the winter.

And as I sat there
behind her
admiring
the beautiful back
of her beautiful head
I wished so badly
that I was
somehow wearing
a pea-colored
olive coat
so that I could be
the yin
to her yang,
        the Cousin Larry
to her Balki Bartokomous,
so that without saying
so much as a word
I could just get up,
walk over to her
and sit in her lap
and slowly

fall asleep
in her arms
as she lovingly petted
my head
like I was a cat.

But
I wasn't wearing
a pea-colored
olive coat,
because
even though
I'm no fashionista,
I'm pretty sure
that pea-colored
olive coats
don't exist
and this left me
all alone
in my seat
with nothing
but my crumby
crotch,
wishing so badly
that I had the courage
to sit down
next to her
and say,

"Excuse me,
I know
I'm not wearing
a pea-colored
olive coat,
but would you mind
possibly
being my corn
muffin?

Would you mind

if I just sat here
next to you
and held your hand
and listened
to Green Day
on my headphones
while you
looked out the window
and daydreamed
about Coffee
Coolattas?

We wouldn't
have to speak.
        We could just
own the air
around
us.

We could
own it
together,
        just you
and I,
and I could
fill my lungs
with you
and you
could fill
your lungs
with me
and if we
do that
        sure
the sun
will still shine down
on us
but maybe
it won't hurt
as much

as it normally
does.

Would you mind
if I wrapped
my silence
around you
like a ribbon?

I think it'd look
really pretty
on you.

I'll wrap
my silence
around you
like a ribbon
and I'll tie it
nice and tight
so it won't fall off,
and if you like it
        and if you wear it
                and if you don't take it off
nothing
will have to be said
and everything
will be understood,
and when
you feel understood
everything feels right
even if
everything is wrong,
and all
anyone really wants
is to be understood.
We're all
just math problems
that want to be
understood
so we can be

solved
so this way
we can be completed
and feel whole.

And most importantly,
        when the train arrives
at Grand Central,
would you mind
untangling yourself
from my frayed
existence
and leave me here
alone
and never see me
again?

And as
you walk away
would you mind
making sure
not to look back
too?
Would you mind
not looking back
so that I'm
so overcome
with grief
that I'll wanna douse
my entire body
in yellow paint
and lay down
in the middle
of the street
and be a human
speed bump?

Would you mind
making me feel
so lonely

that I wanna die?
I don't feel
lonely
ever.
        Not even
a little bit,
and if you don't feel
lonely
ever,
        not even
a little bit,
I'm pretty sure
that means
you're not
real
and I really
wanna be
real.

I wanna really
be real.

I wanna really, really, really
wanna
zigazig
        ahhhhh ...
so slam my body down
and wind it
all around.

Would you mind
doing that
for me?

Would you mind
slamming my body down
and winding it
all around?

I know

it's a lot to ask,
        but at the same time,
it's really not.

It's really not
at all."

I wished
I had the courage
to sit down next to her
and say
all those things
        (except for maybe
the Spice Girls
thing)
but I didn't,
so instead
I just sat there
and dusted
the corn muffin crumbs
off my crotch
and then the train arrived
at Grand Central
and she got up
and left
and disappeared
into the crowd
and I didn't know
        what to do with myself
so I went
to Zaro's Bakery
and I bought myself
another corn muffin,
and buying myself
another corn muffin
made me happy
again.

It made me happy
again

because the corn muffin
was tasty
and it made me happy
again
because it was just nice
to be in good
company
again
too.

Then I walked
out of Grand Central
and went
on my way,
content
and relieved
to be knowing
that for the next
three or four minutes
the sun
wasn't going to
hurt as much
as it normally
did.

… You know what?

I bet she
had
just gone
snorkeling.

the universe told me so

I'm going to be
alone
for awhile.

The universe
told me so.

He tells me so
all the time.

He puts his hand
on my shoulder
the same way
a father
trying to console
his son would,
and he'll say shit
like,
"I see you looking at
that cute redhead
in the skinny jeans
over there
but I wouldn't
if I were you.
You're going to be
alone
for awhile,
remember?"

Then I'm like,
"Aw … yeah.
Okay …"
and then I
hang my head
and look at my shoes
and they look so ragged
that I always think
to myself,

Man,
I really
need to buy
some new shoes.

But
one day
there was this
really cute girl
at the gas station
and she was pumping
her own gas
and as she pumped
her own gas
she was leaning
on the pump
with one hand
and was slightly
bent over
and sticking her ass out
and holy shit
did she have an ass
that I just wanted
to stick my face
into.
So much so
I imagined myself
getting into
a car accident
on purpose
and instead
of my airbag deploying
the really cute girl's ass,
and only her ass,
shoots out
of my steering wheel
and my face
smashes into it
at 100 miles per hour
and I break my nose

and there's blood everywhere
and I'm missing
some of my teeth
but my face
is so far
and deep
into that perfect ass
of hers
that I don't even
care.

I had to go inside
to pay
because the pump
wasn't reading
my debit card
but I told myself,
        I said,
                Fuck the universe.
When I come
back outside
I'm going to ask
that girl out
because I think
she's really cute
and because
I wanna stick my face
in her ass.
        But whatever I do
I'm pretty sure
I shouldn't tell her
that I wanna stick my face
in her ass.
I think I should leave
that part out
for now.
Maybe just save it.
Save it for,
    like,
the second date

or something.

And I thought
that was a good plan
so I hurried inside
and got in
a small line.
There was
a Hindu guy
working the counter
and he looked miserable
and I felt sorry for him
because it was
as hot as balls in there
but even so
all I could think about
was getting out of there
and talking to the cute girl
with the really nice
ass
and then maybe,
possibly,
someday
sticking my face
in her really nice
ass.

It was my turn
to pay
and the miserable-looking
Hindu guy
punched in my total
and told me to swipe
my card.

I did
but it didn't go through.

"... Try again,"
he said.

I did
but it didn't go through.

"… Try again,"
he said.

I did
but it didn't go through.

"… Try again,"
he said.

I did
but it didn't go through.

But this time
he didn't tell me
to try again.

The Hindu guy
grabbed the debit card
out of my hand
and, from the most
awkward angle
imaginable,
he swiped my card
from behind his
cash register
and, in the one,
fluent swipe
he made,
my card went
right through.

I stood there
and felt
really stupid.

I felt emasculated
by what

he had done
to me.

I felt as if
a woman had just
ordered for me
at a really expensive
and classy
restaurant.

I was embarrassed
and I could hear
my balls
rolling around
on the floor.
I looked for them
real quick
but all I saw
were some dust bunnies
and two nickels
that I wanted to
pick up
but I didn't.
I didn't
pick them up
because I was scared
that if I bent over
everyone in line
behind me
would've looked up my skirt
and seen my vagina.

I took my card
and I hung my head
and I looked at my shoes
and they looked so ragged
that I couldn't help
but think to myself,
    Man,
        I really

need to buy
some new shoes.

When I walked
back outside
the cute girl was gone
and so was
her really nice ass
and, even though
I knew that I wasn't going to
ask her out
without my balls,
her leaving
still really hurt
for some reason.

It really,
really
hurt.

Then
the universe came
and put his arm
around my shoulder
and he said,
        "I'm sorry
I had to do that
to you in there
but I had to make sure
you wouldn't
ask her out,
        and I'm sorry to say this
to you again
but you're going to be
alone
for awhile,
and I know
it's not easy
and I know
this isn't what

you wanna hear
but you're not
ready yet.
The truth is
you need to suffer
a little more.
The truth is
you need to be alone
a little longer,
but the good news is
all that suffering
and all that loneliness
will make your heart
bigger
and stronger
and with your heart
bigger
and stronger
you'll go on
to do something
much greater
and much more important
than just killing time
by sticking your face
in some really cute girl's
ass,
and you know
you can do something
much greater
and much more important
than just killing time
by sticking your face
in some really cute girl's
ass.

I'm the universe,
        so just trust me.
I know what I'm doing."

And for the first time

I did,
but I was still
really sad
so I went shopping
and bought myself
a new pair
of shoes
because if I'm
going to be
looking at them
for a little longer
at least now
I understand
that I deserve something
a little bit nicer
to look
at.

… I still have no idea
where my balls are
though

but I'm pretty sure
that's the way
the universe
wants it.

someday i'm going to marry Katy Perry

Someday
I'm going to marry
Katy Perry.

Just wait,
you'll see.

What's that you ask?
Isn't she already married?
Yeah.
So?
She's married
to that crappy
British comedian,
        what's his name?
Randall?
Huh?
What's that
you say?
It's Russell?
Oh.
Well, whatever.
I'm sure
they'll get divorced.
In fact I know
they will.
I have faith.
I know that probably sounds horrible
and I know my poor Katy
will probably be heartbroken
over it all
when it eventually happens
but I also know
that she and Randall
splitting
is ultimately for the best.
Besides,
I'll be there for her.

I'll make her feel better.
I'm not a comedian
per se
but I can make her laugh
too.

I'll tell her jokes.
I'll be like,
"Katy,
how do you get a dog
to stop humping your leg?"

"How?"
she'll ask me.

"Pick him up
and start sucking his dick,"
I'll reply
with perfect comedic timing.

And then she'll laugh
and then I'll laugh
and we'll laugh together
so hard
that we'll fall asleep
in each other's arms.

That will be the beginning
of our courtship
and it wouldn't take long
after that
for her to see
what a stand-up guy
I am.
I would drive us
to romantic places
with scenic views
in my dented '96 Geo Prism.
I'd take her out to dinner
whenever I could afford it.

I'd slow dance
with her to Sam Cooke
and Ritchie Valens.
I'd even leave little love notes
around
for her to find
and they'd say adorable shit like,
"I'll be thinking of you
all day today,"
or
"You farted in your sleep
last night
and I thought it was really cute.
xoxoxo"

In a little over a year
we'd surely be married
and I'd be the happiest man alive
because I'd get to take care of
Katy
for the rest of her life.
I still live with my parents
but I'm sure they wouldn't mind
Katy moving in with us.
They're cool like that.
We'd be one, big,
happy family.
Just me,
Katy,
my mom and dad,
my two cats,
and of course her cat,
Kitty Purry.
It'd be great.
Plus,
I don't want to toot
my own horn
but I'd be the greatest lover
she ever had too.
(Toot,

toot!)
I'd seduce
my beautiful Katy-bear
every night
to make sure
all her deepest
physical desires
were always met …

"Hey baby,"
I'd say to her seductively.
"I know you're probably
still full
from all that Hamburger Helper
I made us for dinner,
and I know the smell
of fresh cat shit
permeating from the litter box
at the foot of the bed
isn't ideal,
but maybe you'd like to make some
sweet,
sweet,
love?
Yeah?
You guess so?
Yeah,
there really isn't anything good
on TV tonight.
Sounds good,
baby.
Let's get at it.
But we need to try
and fuck quietly.
My parents are asleep
right next door."

Ya see?
Katy would be happier
than she'd ever been

in her whole life.
She'd totally forget about
what's his name,
　　Randall?
Russell you say?
Oh whatever.
And to answer
your question,
　　no,
I'm not deliberately
forgetting his name
just to belittle him
like he's not important enough
to remember.
I'm not immature
like that.

　　Anyway,
Katy would be so happy
living with me
in my parents' house
and with all our cats
that she'd never want
to leave my side.
Not even
to go out on tour
or to go record
a new hit album.
But don't worry.
I wouldn't let that happen.
I'd be really supportive
of her career.
I'd remind her of her gift
and that she needs to share it
with the world
because she and her songs
make so many people
happy.

So ya see?

I'd be a really good
husband,
and Katy and I
would have a great life
together,

and it'd be
beautiful,
and it'd be
wonderful,
and it'd be
scary,

and it'd be
difficult
at times
too
because
true love
comes broken.

It is not something
you fall into
and hold on to
but rather
it is always
continually
being built
from the ground up,
constructed from
the collective rubble
and remains
of two,
separate,
lost souls.

It is hard work,
true love,

a gamble

you don't
leave to chance,

and as long
as you know this
and grasp this firmly
with all your heart
and with all ten
of your fingers,

and as long
as you are bold enough
and strong enough
and willing enough
to painstakingly
build it
brick by brick,
then you already
have more to offer a woman
than most of the richest men
in the world.

Someday
I'm going to marry
Katy Perry,

    and not only that,

I'm going to hold on to her
too.

Just wait
and see,
Randall.
Just wait
and see.

xoxoxoxo

i know a great place where you can rent a bear costume for pretty cheap

Fuck it.

That's what I say.

These days
are your days,

    your days
and no one else's.

Not your mom's.
Not your dad's.
Not your brother's or sister's.
Not your dog's.
Not your goldfish's.
Not Snuffy's, or Al's, or Leo's,
or Little Moe with the gimpy leg's,
or Cheeks', or Bony Bob's,
or Cliff's.

No.

These days
are your days,

baby.

Don't be
bullied out
of them
by hatred
or fear
or rancor
or the damning,
snarling
pillars
of society.

If you wanna
wear a bear costume
while you run errands
around town,
        say fuck it,
and wear a bear costume
while you run errands
around town.

If you wanna
fuck men
up their asses
for the rest
of your life,
        say fuck it,
and fuck men
up their asses
for the rest
of your life.

If you wanna
get a tattoo
on your inner thigh
of a squirrel
who's reaching
for your nuts,
        say fuck it,
and get a tattoo
on your inner thigh
of a squirrel
who's reaching
for your nuts.

Just do it,
        and do it
beautifully,
and
unapologetically.

If you're going to

wear a bear costume
while you run errands
around town,
then rock
the ever-loving shit
out of that bear costume
so goddamn hard
that the 60-year-old lady
working behind the counter
at the post office
contemplates
getting one
for herself.

If you're going to
fuck men
up their asses
for the rest of your life,
then fuck them
so long
and so hard
and so deep
and so good
that it leaves
your dick winded
and shriveled
and their asses
so beaten red and sore
that they have to cancel
that mountain biking trip
they've been planning
since spring
and that they were really
looking forward
to.

And if you're going
to get a tattoo
on your inner thigh
of a squirrel

who's reaching
for your nuts,
then get your balls
tattooed
to look like acorns
so then it *really* looks like
the squirrel
on your inner thigh
is reaching
for some nuts.

In five days
I'll be 27 years old.

Just yesterday
I was six years old
and secretly melting crayons
in the radiator
of my first grade classroom
when the teacher
wasn't looking
because I liked the smell
and thought
the crayons looked prettier
when they were
melted and
deformed.

The other kids didn't understand
why I was doing
what I was doing
but that was okay
because I understood
why I was doing
what I was doing.

You don't need
to explain yourself
to the world.
Doing so

would just be a waste
of time.

This poor world
is full of
poor, mutilated
assholes,

assholes
who have been hurt
and who don't want to hurt
any more than they
already do
so they wander the streets
with their bankrupt hearts
and their narrow minds
ready to scratch and claw and tear
anything unfamiliar
and new
and beautiful
like a mean,
starving,
scarred,
crazy son of a bitch
stray cat
with nothing left
to lose,

and they will
try
to slash through
your spirits
and they will
try
to scratch and claw and tear
through you
the same way
they scratch and claw and tear
through the world,

but don't give,
don't bend,
don't change.

What makes you
different
is what
truly
makes you
beautiful.

It takes courage
to be unsung,
to be the minority,
to pee into the wind
with your eyes open.
Sure by doing so
you may get
a few drops of piss
in your eye
but that's okay
because pee is sterile
and because
as you're peeing
into the wind
with your eyes open,
    as you're beautifully
    being
    yourself,
that is when
you'll make the most
wonderful
and amazing
and fulfilling
discoveries
of your entire
life.

And when you do
discover something,

don't hesitate.
Grab it.
Seize it
by the base
of its balls,
because if something
makes you happy,
and as long as it
doesn't hurt
or impede
the rights
of anyone else
along the way,
you just need to say,
"Fuck it,"
and then
do it,

and then fuck
everyone else
along the way
who doesn't
get it,

because, guess what?

They're not invited
to the awesome,
end of the semester,
cool kid,
pool party
that is
your life.

Your life,

and no one
else's.

epitaph

"Sophomorically wise,
Idiotically brilliant."

That's what I want it to say
on my gravestone.

I used to want my gravestone to read,
"Man, what a monster cock he had ..."
but I didn't think anyone
would believe it.

Plus,
I want to have kids someday
and after I die
I'd like for them to occasionally come
and visit my grave
and I just feel like they'd be
a lot less inclined
to come visit me if I had
"Man, what a monster cock he had ..."
etched on to my tombstone.

But,
maybe if I did a good enough job,
maybe if I was a decent enough dad,
they'd still come and visit my grave
regardless of whether I had that
engraved
on there
or not.

I figure that if I can get my kids
to come and visit my grave
after I die
at all,
even just once,
then maybe my life
wasn't a complete failure.

Maybe I wasn't
a complete fucking fuck up
as a human being.

We all just want to feel special
and we would all love to be adored
by the entire world
but maybe you don't need
the entire world to find you special.
Maybe you don't need
the entire world to adore you.
Maybe all you need
in the end
is a handful
of people
that will still come
and visit your grave
even if you have
"Man, what a monster cock he had ..."
engraved on your tombstone.

Maybe that would be a victory
for me in itself,
        and maybe,
just maybe
someone would actually believe
I had a monster cock
too.

Man,
that'd be awesome.

Acknowledgements

This book would cease to be if it weren't for Mom, Dad, Aunt Alice, Green Day, Ralph, Matilda, Charlie Chaplin, Coke Zero, Hank, and, of course, my best friend Dave (a.k.a. Jerry Revere) who once told me, "Trust me, bro. You just need to keep at it. I promise you the world isn't going to be ready for the work that comes out of that basement in Trumbull, Connecticut." Thank you, Dave.

About the Author

Calvero currently lives in his parents' basement with his two cats, Ralph and Matilda. That sentence is also the pick-up line he uses when he's trying to pick up girls at a bar, but, surprisingly, it never gets him any action whatsoever. Calvero is one cat away from becoming a crazy cat guy and if that isn't bad enough he works with cats at a cat hospital too. When he's not writing or working he is more often than not eating Taco Bell, daydreaming about hunting ghosts, daydreaming about Taco Bell when he's not eating Taco Bell, or screaming in frustration at whatever video game he is currently addicted to. He has been published in several online literary journals and thinks you should buy this book so he can finally move out of his parents' basement.

HELL
PRESS
UNIVERSITY OF HELL PRESS

CPSIA information can be obtained at www.ICGtesting.com
Printed in the USA
LVOW05s1956011013

354951LV00005B/428/P